Advertising

Other books in the Introducing Issues
with Opposing Viewpoints series:

INTRODUCING ISSUES WITH OPPOSING VIEWPOINTS®

Advertising

Eleanor Stanford, *Book Editor*

Christine Nasso, *Publisher*
Elizabeth Des Chenes, *Managing Editor*

GREENHAVEN PRESS

An imprint of Thomson Gale, a part of The Thomson Corporation

THOMSON

GALE

Detroit • New York • San Francisco • New Haven, Conn. • Waterville, Maine • London

LIBRARY OF CONGRESS CATALOGING-IN-PUBLICATION DATA

Advertising / Eleanor Stanford, book editor.
    p. cm. — (Introducing issues with opposing viewpoints)
    Includes bibliographical references and index.
    ISBN 13: 978-0-7377-3572-7 (lib : alk. paper)
    ISBN 10: 0-7377-3572-4 (lib : alk. paper)
    1. Advertising. 2. Advertising and children. I. Stanford, Eleanor. II. Series.
    HF5823.A1683 2007
    659.1—dc22
 	
                                                                                       2006043596

Printed in the United States of America

Contents

Foreword

Indulging in a wide spectrum of ideas, beliefs, and perspectives is a critical cornerstone of democracy. After all, it is often debates over differences of opinion, such as whether to legalize abortion, how to treat prisoners, or when to enact the death penalty, that shape our society and drive it forward. Such diversity of thought is frequently regarded as the hallmark of a healthy and civilized culture. As the Reverend Clifford Schutjer of the First Congregational Church in Mansfield, Ohio, declared in a 2001 sermon, "Surrounding oneself with only like-minded people, restricting what we listen to or read only to what we find agreeable is irresponsible. Refusing to entertain doubts once we make up our minds is a subtle but deadly form of arrogance." With this advice in mind, Introducing Issues with Opposing Viewpoints books aim to open readers' minds to the critically divergent views that comprise our world's most important debates.

Introducing Issues with Opposing Viewpoints simplifies for students the enormous and often overwhelming mass of material now available via print and electronic media. Collected in every volume is an array of opinions that captures the essence of a particular controversy or topic. Introducing Issues with Opposing Viewpoints books embody the spirit of nineteenth-century journalist Charles A. Dana's axiom: "Fight for your opinions, but do not believe that they contain the whole truth, or the only truth." Absorbing such contrasting opinions teaches students to analyze the strength of an argument and compare it to its opposition. From this process readers can inform and strengthen their own opinions, or be exposed to new information that will change their minds. Introducing Issues with Opposing Viewpoints is a mosaic of different voices. The authors are statesmen, pundits, academics, journalists, corporations, and ordinary people who have felt compelled to share their experiences and ideas in a public forum. Their words have been collected from newspapers, journals, books, speeches, interviews, and the Internet, the fastest growing body of opinionated material in the world.

Introducing Issues with Opposing Viewpoints shares many of the well-known features of its critically acclaimed parent series, Opposing Viewpoints. The articles are presented in a pro/con format, allowing readers to absorb divergent perspectives side by side. Active reading questions preface each viewpoint, requiring the student to approach the material thoughtfully and carefully. Useful charts, graphs, and cartoons supplement each article. A thorough introduction provides readers with crucial background on an issue. An annotated bibliography points the reader toward articles, books, and Web sites that contain additional information on the topic. An appendix of organizations to contact contains a wide variety of charities, nonprofit organizations, political groups, and private enterprises that each hold a position on the issue at hand. Finally, a comprehensive index allows readers to locate content quickly and efficiently.

Introducing Issues with Opposing Viewpoints is also significantly different from Opposing Viewpoints. As the series title implies, its presentation will help introduce students to the concept of opposing viewpoints, and learn to use this material to aid in critical writing and debate. The series' four-color, accessible format makes the books attractive and inviting to readers of all levels. In addition, each viewpoint has been carefully edited to maximize a reader's understanding of the content. Short but thorough viewpoints capture the essence of an argument. A substantial, thought-provoking essay question placed at the end of each viewpoint asks the student to further investigate the issues raised in the viewpoint, compare and contrast two authors' arguments, or consider how one might go about forming an opinion on the topic at hand. Each viewpoint contains sidebars that include at-a-glance information and handy statistics. A Facts About section located in the back of the book further supplies students with relevant facts and figures.

Following in the tradition of the Opposing Viewpoints series, Greenhaven Press continues to provide readers with invaluable exposure to the controversial issues that shape our world. As John Stuart Mill once wrote: "The only way in which a human being can make some approach to knowing the whole of a subject is by hearing what can be said about it by persons of every variety of opinion and studying all modes in which it can be looked at by every character of mind. No wise man ever acquired his wisdom in any mode but this." It is to this principle that Introducing Issues with Opposing Viewpoints books are dedicated.

Introduction

"Schools should not be in the business of providing a venue for advertisers to promote their wares."

—Megan Santosus, Editor, *CIO Magazine*

Imagine going to a school named not after a town, geographical landmark, or historical figure, but after a corporation. In Philadelphia, such a school opened in September 2006. The School of the Future, as the public high school is currently known, is its working title; the actual name of the school is available for purchase for $5 million. Names of individual classrooms can also be bought for smaller sums.

Advertising has made increasing inroads into public schools for several decades. Advertisements for Burger King, Wendy's, and other brand-name establishments have graced the sides of school buses; similar images for Kellogg's Pop-Tarts, Frosted Flakes, and Lay's Potato Chips have appeared on free textbook covers handed out to students. Other advertising space has been sold on school rooftops to companies such as 7UP and Dr Pepper sodas, or displayed on banners in hallways. Still other companies such as Coca-Cola and Taco Bell have entered into agreements with a school or school district, allowing their product to be exclusively sold in the cafeteria and break rooms. Corporations have also sponsored contests and incentive programs in schools, rewarding students for selling their products with prizes such as pizza, cash, or trips; magazine drives are a common example of this practice.

Ingeniously, advertisers have even bought space within the school curriculum itself. Author Steven Manning has reported on exercise books that teach third graders math by having them count Tootsie Rolls, and business courses that teach students the value of work by showing them how McDonald's restaurants are run. In another example, feminine hygiene companies or condom manufacturers, such as Tampax or Trojan, may produce videos and other educational materials for health classes. Commercialism further infiltrates American

The School of the Future, in Philadelphia, will be named after whichever company donates $5 million.

public schools via television advertisements inserted directly into the classroom. This method came into its own in 1989 with the introduction of Channel One, a company that produces a daily twelve-minute news program along with a two-minute commercial segment. In exchange for airing the program and the advertising for three years, Channel One will provide schools with a satellite dish, a cable hookup, and a television monitor for each classroom. Corporate-sponsored educational materials and programs such as these represent new and powerful ways to mesh advertising with academia.

All of these forms of advertising, and Channel One in particular, have long provided fodder for debate in American society. The concept of allowing advertising in schools, and particularly the concept of using a high school's name as a vehicle for product advertisement, raises questions about the boundaries of advertising. Some groups, such as the antiadvertisement organization Commercial Alert, believe that schools should be ad-free zones. "Schools exist to teach children how to read, write, and think," Commercial Alert asserts, "not to shop." For Gary Ruskin, executive director of the organization, the naming of Philadelphia's School of the Future is an example of commercialism gone too far. "It is a sign in the decline of our values that we name things not after our heroes or history, but after corporations

Whether or not students should be exposed to advertising during the school day is a matter of debate.

with the deepest pockets," he said. Furthermore, exposing students to advertising in schools concerns those who believe entering a for-profit product into the educational environment corrupts what should be objective academic information. Finally, the practice is perceived as being unfair to children, who essentially become a captive audience for advertisers. As high school principal Joshua Segal wrote in October 2004 in the *New York Times,* "It is unseemly for a school district to sell its space for the pittance it receives. It has abandoned inspiration for commercialization."

Proponents of allowing advertising in schools, on the other hand, claim that the reward for schools is often much more than a pittance. Schools that make deals with advertisers are often the recipients of new computer equipment, upgraded lab tools, or improved athletic facilities. In 1998, for example, Hillsboro School District near Portland, Oregon, with approximately nineteen thousand students, signed a twelve-year exclusive contract with Coca-Cola that won the school about 30 percent of the sales revenue from soda sold on school property plus a three-hundred-thousand-dollar upfront cash payment and a million-dollar-all-weather playing field. For particularly poor schools, such

David Horsey. Copyright © 2002 by the *Seattle Post-Intelligencer,* Tribune Media Services. Reproduced by permission.

Some schools allow advertising on their campuses because the extra revenue allows them to purchase laptops, lab equipment, and other educational resources.

arrangements can be very lucrative, winning them equipment and facilities that they otherwise would be unable to afford. Furthermore, it is commonly argued that through the multitude of media digested by children—from television to the Internet to magazines—students are going to see these advertisements anyway; they may as well be reaping benefits for their educational environment as they do so. Still others argue that corporate backers of education need not dilute the quality of education, pointing to certain corporate programs that seek to enrich student performance. The Pizza Hut "BOOK IT!" program is an example of one such program. In BOOK IT! students can earn a certificate for a free personal pan pizza by reading a certain number of books. According to Pizza Hut, the program has reached 22 million students in kindergarten through sixth grade in fifty thousand schools since 1985. Defenders of advertising in schools, such as Robert N.C. Nix III, a Philadelphia official, feel that the benefits of advertising far outweigh the pitfalls. Says Nix: "It's nice to have a good deal where you get your fields improved, you get much-needed financial help, and you get a great facility in your park system." Indeed, schools and students are the only winners when advertisers enter schools, according to those who favor in-school advertising.

As advertisers adopt new tactics in schools and other venues, their practices continue to generate controversy over how much advertising should be allowed to permeate everyday life and if it is a force of good or bad. The writers featured in *Introducing Issues with Opposing Viewpoints: Advertising* debate the various effects of advertising on people and society, as well as possible solutions for dealing with the complex issues the topic raises.

Chapter 1

Is Advertising Harmful?

Teachers, parents, government officials, and others hotly debate the effect of advertising on children.

Advertising Is Too Prevalent in American Society

Gary Ruskin and Juliet B. Schor

"Corporations have . . . proliferate[d] advertising into nearly every nook and cranny of life."

Advertising has infiltrated nearly all aspects of American life, Gary Ruskin and Juliet B. Schor argue in the following viewpoint. Corporations have become increasingly powerful, and as a result many institutions, such as churches, schools, and government, have become commercialized. Advertising has encouraged materialism, stifled public discussion, increased disease, and polluted the environment. The authors hope advertising can be curbed in the United States as it has been in other countries.

Ruskin is executive director of the non-profit organization Commercial Alert. Schor, author of *Born to Buy*, is a professor of sociology at Boston College.

AS YOU READ, CONSIDER THE FOLLOWING QUESTIONS:

1. According to the authors, what is "place-based" advertising and "product placement"?

Gary Ruskin and Juliet B. Schor, "Every Nook and Cranny: The Dangerous Spread of Commercialized Culture (25 Years of Monitoring the Multinationals)," *Multinational Monitor*, vol. 26, January/February 2005, pp. 20–23. Copyright © 2005 by Essential Information, Inc. Reproduced by permission.

2. What ruling did the Supreme Court make in 1976 regarding commercial speech?
3. What were the findings of a 2004 poll conducted by Yankelovich Partners?

While advertising has long been an element in the circus of U.S. life, not until recently has it been recognized as having political or social merit. For nearly two centuries, advertising (lawyers call it commercial speech) was not protected by the U.S. Constitution. The U.S. Supreme Court ruled in 1942 that states could regulate commercial speech at will. But in 1976, the Court granted constitutional protection to commercial speech. Corporations have used this new right of speech to proliferate advertising into nearly every nook and cranny of life.

In Schools, in Movies, on Buses, and on Trains

During most of the twentieth century, there was little advertising in schools. That changed in 1989, when Chris Whittle's Channel One enticed schools to accept advertising, by offering to loan TV sets to classrooms. Each school day, Channel One features at least two minutes of ads, and 10 minutes of news, fluff, banter and quizzes. The program is shown to about 8 million children in 12,000 schools. . . .

Energy, candy, personal care products, even automobile manufacturers have entered the classroom with "sponsored educational materials"—that is, ads in the guise of free "curricula.". . .

Advertisers have long relied on 30-second TV spots to deliver messages to mass audiences. During the 1990s, the impact of these ads began to drop off, in part because viewers simply clicked to different programs during ads. In response, many advertisers began to place ads elsewhere, leading to "ad creep"—the spread of ads throughout social space and cultural institutions. Whole new marketing subspecialties developed, such as "place-based" advertising, which coerces captive viewers to watch video ads. Examples include ads before movies, ads on buses and trains in cities (Chicago, Milwaukee and Orlando), and CNN's Airport channel. Video ads are also now common on ATMs, gas pumps, in convenience stores and doctors' offices.

Another form of ad creep is "product placement," in which advertisers pay to have their product included in movies, TV shows, museum exhibits, or other forms of media and culture. Product placement is thought to be more effective than the traditional 30-second ad because it sneaks by the viewer's critical faculties. Product placement has recently occurred in novels, and children's books. Some U.S. TV programs (*American Idol, The Restaurant, The Apprentice*) and movies (*Minority Report, Cellular*) are so full of product placement that they resemble infomercials. By contrast, many European nations, such as Austria, Germany, Norway and the United Kingdom, ban or sharply restrict product placement on television. . . .

Students are exposed to TV advertisements on Channel One, which in turn provides schools with televisions and other equipment.

Boligan. Cagle Cartoons, Inc. Reproduced by permission.

Advertising's Harmful Effects

Because the phenomenon of commercialism has become so ubiquitous, it is not surprising that its effects are as well. Perhaps most alarming has been the epidemic of marketing-related diseases afflicting people in the United States, and especially children, such as obesity, type 2 diabetes and smoking-related illnesses. Each day, about 2,000 U.S. children begin to smoke, and about one-third of them will die from

Product Placement on Television Programs

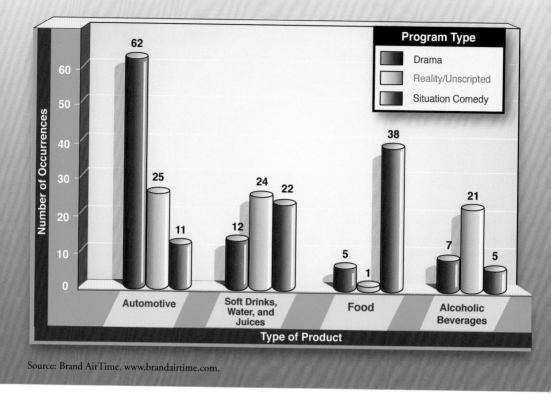

Source: Brand AirTime, www.brandairtime.com.

tobacco-related illnesses. Children are inundated with advertising for high-calorie junk food and fast food, and, predictably, 15 percent of U.S. children aged 6 to 19 are now overweight.

Excessive commercialism is also creating a more materialistic populace. In 2003, the annual UCLA survey of incoming college freshmen found that the number of students who said it was a very important or essential life goal to "develop a meaningful philosophy of life" fell to an all-time low of 39 percent, while succeeding financially has increased to a 13-year high, at 74 percent. High involvement in consumer culture has been shown to be a significant cause of depression, anxiety, low self-esteem and psychosomatic complaints in children, findings which parallel similar studies of materialism among teens and adults. Other impacts are more intangible. A 2004 poll by Yankelovich Partners found that 61 percent of the U.S. public "feel that the amount of marketing and advertising is out of control," and

65 percent "feel constantly bombarded with too much advertising and marketing." Is advertising diminishing our sense of general well-being? Perhaps. . . .

Advertising Harms the Natural and Social Environment

This imbalance also affects the natural environment. The additional consumption created by the estimated $265 billion that the advertising industry will spend in 2004 will also yield more pollution, natural resource destruction, carbon dioxide emissions and global warming.

Finally, advertising has also contributed to a narrowing of the public discourse, as advertising-driven media grow ever more timid. Sometimes it seems as if we live in an echo chamber, a place where corporations speak and everyone else listens.

Governments at all levels have failed to address these impacts. . . .

However, as commercialism grows more intrusive, public distaste for it will likely increase, as will political support for restricting it. In the long run, we believe this hopeful trend will gather strength.

EVALUATING THE AUTHORS' ARGUMENTS:

The authors of this viewpoint blame advertising for an increase in materialism, pollution, and illness. What do you think? Is advertising solely responsible, or do consumers share some of the blame? Explain your reasoning.

Advertising Is Not Too Prevalent in American Society

Wall Street Journal

"Ads are an essential ingredient in the free-enterprise system."

In the following viewpoint the editors of the *Wall Street Journal* argue that although advertising has become more prevalent in American society, it helps more people than it hurts. For example, most people are employed by some type of company that uses advertising to make money, they point out. They explain why most advertising is a normal part of modern American culture. While certain types of advertising have become more underhanded, the authors conclude the best defense is for the consumer to view these ads with a critical eye.

AS YOU READ, CONSIDER THE FOLLOWING QUESTIONS:

1. Why did two stories from the *Wall Street Journal* strike the authors as startling?

2. How do the authors use the TiVo example to strengthen their argument?
3. What occurred in the "payola scandal" of 1959 that the authors mention?

Two separate news stories in [the April 19, 2005] *Wall Street Journal* caught our attention for the same reason. A front-page article was headlined "Advice for Sale: How Companies Pay TV Experts for On-Air Product Mentions." Elsewhere in the paper was a report with the headline "Satellite Radio Latches On to Ads." Each story was startling in its own way. Ostensibly neutral consumer experts on TV news-show segments may in fact have a business relationship with the companies whose products they recommend. Listeners who fled to satellite radio to escape commercial-radio advertising soon may have nowhere left to run.

Almost Everyone Benefits from Ads

Startling, but not surprising. Lenin once characterized all human intercourse with the phrase "everything is politics." These days, it can seem, everything is advertising.

In general, we can't complain. Ads are an essential ingredient in the free-enterprise system. Virtually everyone who has a job, including employees of this newspaper, benefits from the commerce that would be impossible if the providers of various services and products could not make their availability known. Even those pesky interruptions for ads on TV wouldn't be avoidable now unless the providers of TiVo-type services had let us know that their gadgets were out there.

Advertising Is a Normal Part of Modern Entertainment

Arguably, association with advertising enjoys more acceptance today than at any time in modern memory. Until fairly recently, for instance, most celebrities wouldn't be caught dead doing paid pitches in the U.S. When actress Brenda Vaccaro made a tampon ad in 1981, she was ridiculed partly because it was widely assumed that a performer who went commercial like that was signaling the end of her real career. After Michael Jackson and a few other performers began doing commercials in the 1980s, folk-rocker Neil Young struck back with the song "This Note's for You" and its sneering lyrics: "Ain't singin' for Pepsi / ain't singin' for Coke / I don't sing for nobody / Makes me look like a joke." Back then, people recognized the taint that he was talking about, even if they weren't quite as worked up about it as Mr. Young was. These days, however, an icon like Robert De Niro can do an American Express ad and nobody bats an eye. We've come a long way, baby.

Yet with most of the pitches of the past, people on the receiving end knew that they were being pitched to. They assumed that there was a clear line between news or honest opinion and paid huckster-

Most Americans have gotten used to the fact that advertisements are a common feature of society.

A man views a digital ad in a Chicago subway. Some believe that advertisements are a normal part of modern American culture.

ism. That's why the so-called payola scandal of 1959 caused such a huge uproar. The revelations about how disc jockeys were being paid by recording companies to play certain songs genuinely shocked and outraged the nation.

We Can Be Cynical but Not Angry

In an age of near-ubiquitous product placement in TV sitcoms and movies, we've grown wiser and more cynical. Now some local and network TV news shows have been outed for not checking to see if the "consumer experts" they offered as unbiased judges were, in effect, advertising products for clients. A dismaying thought, yet more cynicism may be the closest emotion to outrage that a jaded public can muster.

Since the average citizen has lost the ability to turn off or turn away from promotions that don't interest him, however, who can blame him for daydreaming of revenge? In the TV consumer-segment fandango, perhaps the IRS will find new fodder: taxes due on the value of undeclared ads covertly planted by a product-maker. As for fans of such segments who never twigged that they might, in fact, be watching plain old ads in a new wrapper, add this update to the basic maxim: caveat viewer.

EVALUATING THE AUTHORS' ARGUMENTS:

The authors of this viewpoint argue that advertising does not threaten American society. The authors of the previous viewpoint disagree. After reading both viewpoints, what is your opinion? Would you support efforts to reduce advertising? If so, what kinds?

Advertising Stereotypes Minorities

"What children think of various ethnic minorities . . . is often influenced by what they see on television programs and advertising."

Hae-Kyong Bang and Bonnie B. Reece

In the following viewpoint Hae-Kyong Bang and Bonnie B. Reece argue that many television commercials portray minorities stereotypically. Certain minorities are often associated with products that make a statement of a group's intelligence or moral character, Bang and Reece assert. These portrayals, the authors contend, negatively influence children's perceptions of both others and themselves. Bang is a professor of marketing at Villanova University, and Reece is a professor of advertising at Michigan State University.

AS YOU READ, CONSIDER THE FOLLOWING QUESTIONS:

1. How many advertisements do Bang and Reece claim the average American child sees each year?
2. In what category of advertisements were blacks most represented, according to the authors?
3. According to Bang and Reece, in what setting are blacks and Asian Americans less likely than Caucasians to be shown?

Hae-Kyong Bang and Bonnie B. Reece, "Minorities in Children's Television Commericals: New, Improved, and Stereotyped," *Journal of Consumer Affairs*, vol. 37, Summer 2003, pp. 42–68. Copyright © 2003 by Basil Blackwell, Ltd. Reproduced by permission of Blackwell Publishers, www.blackwell-synergy.com.

A dvertising bombards children in America. The average child in the U.S. may see more than 20,000 commercials per year in addition to some television programs that are actually hour-long commercials for toys and games. American children aged 2 through 11 watch television for 19 hours and 40 minutes per week. Watching television is what children do most when they are not sleeping, and, more significantly, they often watch unaccompanied by adults. Thus, although other socialization agents such as schools, peers, or parents influence children's cognitive development, television, including commercials, has become an important part of the socialization process.

By transmitting selective images and ideas, television commercials not only teach young consumers to buy and consume certain products, but they also teach children to accept certain beliefs and values. Thus, what children think of various ethnic minorities such as Blacks, Hispanics, or Asian Americans is often influenced by what they see on television programs and advertising. According to social learning theory, people learn certain beliefs and behaviors based on their observation of other people's behaviors. Thus, if a television commercial shows a bright Black student being praised for outstanding academic performance after he or she eats a Carnation breakfast bar, young viewers, particularly children of color, may believe that they can perform as well as the model in the ad if they have the breakfast bar.

Likewise, . . . constant exposures to a specific image of an object can lead to distorted beliefs about the object. Thus, if children are repeatedly exposed to certain portrayals of an ethnic group, they may develop corresponding beliefs about the group. For instance, if children consistently see Asian Americans playing roles of technicians or mathematicians on television, they may learn to believe that Asian Americans are smart people. This impact can be even greater if the children live without much meaningful contact with ethnic groups other than their own. . . .

Problems with Representation

The [findings of our] study showed that some problematic patterns persist [regarding advertising and minorities]. These patterns may affect minority consumers' views of their role in society. First, certain

Teenagers who watch television increasingly want to see people like themselves portrayed in programming and advertising.

aspects of quantitative representation remain an issue. For instance, when the number of models was analyzed, only Blacks were over represented among minority groups. Likewise, when it came to single ethnic group representation, the study found that minorities were still seldom shown without a Caucasian model in the ad, while Caucasians were much more frequently shown as a single ethnic group. It is easy to pick out models of color because they rarely appear, but harder to see their absence in all-Caucasian commercials. If children learn to behave in a certain way by watching other people behave, as social learning theory suggests, children of color in particular may not have as many opportunities to learn about interaction within their group. Similarly Caucasian children may learn to believe that other ethnic groups are just like them, and thus fail to respect differences that exist among other ethnic groups. . . .

Skewed Portrayals

A second problem was found in the continued stereotyping of certain minorities portrayed in children's television advertising. Some current portrayals of minorities with a clear association with certain

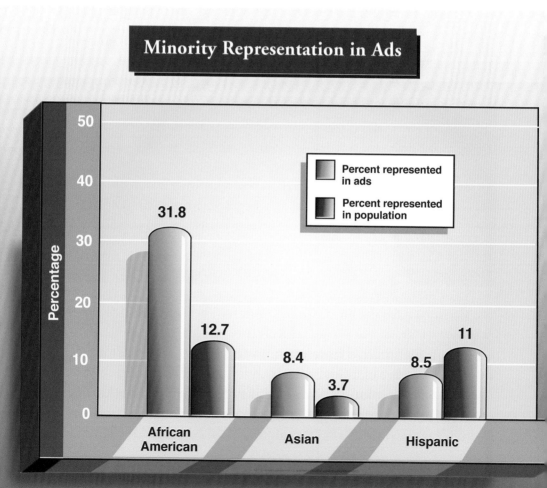

Minority Representation in Ads

product categories may perpetuate stereotypes. For instance, our study found that Blacks were still more likely to be featured in food commercials than any other ethnic group, while simultaneously being the least likely to be featured in toy commercials. This striking association with the food category was not found with any other ethnic groups. . . . This kind of continued stereotyping can unduly influence children's beliefs about certain minorities. The under-representation of Black children in toy commercials may cultivate a belief that Black children are not "mainstream" enough to appear in all types of commercials.

Similar to the findings by product category, the study found that Blacks and Asian Americans were less likely than Caucasians to be shown in a home setting or in family relationships. Again, . . . the absence of portrayals in these settings may contribute to a stereotype that many Black people do not have strong family ties or that many Asian American parents are too busy at their workplace to have family time at home.

The study also found that while children and teenagers accounted for the majority of the models of all ethnic groups, which was expected for children's advertising, Caucasian adult representation was much higher than the minority adult representation. This may lead to a perception that minority children are left unsupervised much more readily than Caucasian children, and that the absence of adults in minority children's life is quite widespread. Thus, in the context of minority children being exposed to the persuasive communications of advertisers, skewed portrayals may have a negative impact on consumers perceptions of other groups as consumers as well as members of society at large.

Implications for Children

The findings have implications for children, both as consumers and members of society at large. Children reported that television is a major learning source. The frequency with which Caucasians appear, and the prominence of their roles, may reinforce the perception that Caucasians are more important than others just because they are the majority. This can have a negative impact on minority children since the importance of their existence in this world is reduced in the world

Asian contestants are featured on the popular reality show Survivor. *How minorities are portrayed on television may enforce certain stereotypes about them.*

of television, therefore potentially harming the child's self-perception. Some prior research emphasizes this concern since studies have shown that Black children were more likely to perceive what they see in advertising as being truthful. A negative impact may also be extended to majority children in some way because their perceived self-importance may be unduly inflated in the world of television. Therefore if a child repeatedly sees a model of his or her ethnic group playing a minor role or major role, it can lead to somewhat unrealistic self-perception. . . . Thus, conscious efforts should be made to portray all ethnic groups fairly and in a non-stereotypical manner so that minority groups are seen as valued consumers well integrated into the society.

EVALUATING THE AUTHORS' ARGUMENTS:

Bang and Reece argue that people make judgments about minorities based on their roles in commercials. Think about commercials you have seen recently. How are minorities presented? Do these roles influence the way you think about a whole group of people? If so, in what way?

Viewpoint

4

Advertisers Are Improving Their Portrayal of Minorities

"The ad industry has come a long way since 1969, when complaints from Mexican Americans forced Frito-Lay's animated Frito Bandito character off the air."

Joan Voight

In the following viewpoint Joan Voight argues that modern advertisers make a conscious effort to avoid stereotyping minorities. Voight claims that as minority groups such as blacks, Hispanics, senior citizens, and gays gain political and economic power, advertisers are forced to show more realistic images of these groups in their commercials. Marketers do not want to run the risk of offending potential consumers, Voight argues. This economic pressure is causing companies to improve the way they portray minorities in ads.

Voight is a reporter for *ADWEEK*.

AS YOU READ, CONSIDER THE FOLLOWING QUESTIONS:

1. According to Mike Wilke, what can make an ad look dated? Why?

2. What percentage of the customer base will be Hispanic, black, and Asian by 2050, according to Voight?
3. What changes has Anheuser-Busch made to its beer ads, as described by the author?

The ad industry has come a long way since 1969, when complaints from Mexican Americans forced Frito-Lay's animated Frito Bandito character off the air. . . .

Marketers rarely admit that ad stereotypes are damaging brands, but some are quietly shifting their strategies. Anheuser-Busch, for instance, has downplayed stereotypical gay humor in its Bud Light ads, focusing instead on relationship quirks between men and women. A few years ago, Detroit largely abandoned car ads showing Hispanic women in skimpy dresses dancing to salsa music. . . .

Ads React to a Changing America

U.S. Census figures indicate that Hispanic, black and Asian consumers will make up about half of the customer base of most U.S. mass-market companies by 2050. Last year, African Americans and Hispanics made up 32% of the U.S. population, and that number is expected to grow. At the same time, baby boomers are changing the perception of older Americans, and gays and lesbians are becoming pop culture trendsetters through TV hits such as *Will and Grace* and *Queer Eye for the Straight Guy.*

"We aren't talking about the fringe audiences anymore," said Mike Wilke, ad consultant and executive director of Commercial Closet, which tracks gay-themed ads. Misuse of stereotypes in ads "can make a brand look dated overnight," he warns.

Stereotypes Are Unavoidable but Harmless

Yet advertising, which tells most of its stories in 30-second bursts, is an industry that trades on stereotypes. "Ads have to telegraphically sum up their characters in a few seconds, and stereotypes are the easiest way to do it," said Katherine Sender, assistant professor of communications at the University of Pennsylvania.

Many recurring stereotypes seem harmless: the clumsy dad, the happy housewife, the handsome gay man, the African American basketball player or musician, the Hispanic soccer player, etc. "What makes the stereotype turn negative is when it alienates the group being portrayed," Sender said. "Whether the portrayal is negative or positive is in the eye of the beholder. It can be really hard for an agency to know which is which." . . .

Showing Sensitivity to Cultural Differences

Many agency executives say they are sensitive to negative stereotypes. Jeff Goodby, principal of Goodby, Silverstein & Partners, San Francisco, said that if a storyline makes fun of a character, an agency will typically be wary of casting a minority actor in the role for fear of being disrespectful. For a Dreyer's Ice Cream ad that aired [in 2003] and centered on a father and son, Goodby directed the actors, who were black, a little differently than he would have if they were white. He and other creative directors say they are careful not to reinforce the negative stereotype of the African American father who can't support his family and is a weak authority figure.

"Rarely in an ad do you see an African American dad being the goofball or the butt of the joke," he said. "We paid more attention to showing that while the son was embarrassed by his wacky inventor dad, he clearly loved his father. We had to make sure the kid did not seem too critical, because that would seem inappropriate in a black family."

Avoiding Stereotypes of the Elderly

Faithfully representing older people in ads is also tricky, given that boomers are revamping the meaning of retirement. John Killpack, brand management director at AARP (formerly the American Association of Retired Persons), declines frequent requests to sponsor golf tournaments because, he says, so few AARP members play golf. (Only 11–12% of people age 45–64 are golfers, and even fewer are found over 65, according to the National Sporting Goods Association.)

Another common ad stereotype is that of the elderly bingo player, a character that North Castle Partners in Stamford, Conn., used in a TV ad for Icebreakers gum [in 2003].

Popular shows such as Will and Grace *(the cast of which is pictured) increasingly feature gay and other previously marginalized characters.*

Steve Garbett, creative director and partner, said the bingo parlor was useful as "a very low-energy setting" that could be enlivened by the breath-freshening gum into "a high-energy place where people make amorous social connections." The client questioned if the ad might be offensive, but agency creatives convinced them it would

Today advertisers try to avoid negatively stereotyping senior citizens for fear of turning away potential customers.

be empowering for seniors to see their peers acting young, said Garbett.

In their work for AARP, creatives at GSD&M in Austin, Texas, learned firsthand what not to do. The most common and offensive stereotypes of seniors, said planning director Rene Huey-Lipton, are that of the frail, scared victim, followed closely by that of the happy, carefree older person made up to look younger. In fact, seniors tend to be "whipsmart, informed and opinionated, far from passive and on the edges of society," she said.

In ads that broke early this year, the agency showed ordinary, casually dressed people in their 50s and 60s telling insurance, healthcare and government executives what to do. "We are turning the passive stereotype on its ear," Killpack noted. . . .

Taking Steps

Some agencies and clients are using formal or informal advisers to get in step, culturally. Some are consulting with minority agencies or reaching out to recruit more minority staffers. But for many shops, such steps are an added bureaucratic layer and an empty exercise in political correctness.

Still, planners and creatives can try to set aside their assumptions and use consumer sessions and research tools to try to understand these groups on an emotional level. "When you study the depth of these consumer segments, you uncover naked emotions you don't expect, which offer raw material for good creative work," said Huey-Lipton. . . .

Advertisers Are Learning That Stereotypes Don't Pay

Advertising and marketing will probably always lean on stereotypes as shorthand devices to get emotional messages across. But the images are getting more challenging to employ. It's easy to see how Frito Bandito and Aunt Jemima would be offensive, but what creative team would worry about showing a prosperous young black man singing Led Zeppelin or an attractive retired couple taking a stroll? . . .

This year, Jaguar is consulting with minority advisers, and Procter & Gamble is conducting research on seniors, according to industry sources. Even Miller Lite and Amstel Light—yes, beer brands—were lauded by gay critics last year for bar ads that effortlessly showed straight and gay people hanging out together.

Soon agencies could find that dodging negative stereotypes is more a matter of economic, than political, correctness.

EVALUATING THE AUTHORS' ARGUMENTS:

In the previous viewpoint the authors discuss social reasons for advertisers to reject commercials that stereotype. In this viewpoint the author discusses economic reasons for advertisers to reject commercials that stereotype. In your opinion, which reason is more compelling? Explain.

Chapter 2

Should Advertising Be Restricted?

Many U.S. cities are blanketed with advertising, causing some to wonder if it should be restricted.

Advertising Should Be Restricted

Ed Ayres

"Dishonest messages are now all around us, in every medium— and I think getting worse."

In the following viewpoint Ed Ayres argues that advertising should be restricted. As advertising becomes more pervasive in our society, he believes it has also become more misleading. Advertisements inappropriately factor into peoples' important decisions, he argues. Moreover, Ayres is concerned that people cannot tell the difference between an advertisement and a factual news report. Ayres suggests that publishers, editors, and media producers should work harder to curb advertisers. Ayres is the editor of *World Watch* magazine, from which this viewpoint was taken.

AS YOU READ, CONSIDER THE FOLLOWING QUESTIONS:
1. What are some of the ways advertising has disguised itself, according to Ayres?
2. What issue does the author have with drug advertisers?
3. What plans does the National Rifle Association have, according to Ayres?

Ed Ayres, "What Happens to Civilization When Its Main Source of Knowledge Is Ads (Note from a Worldwatcher)?" *World Watch,* vol. 17, March/April 2004, pp. 3–5. Copyright © 2004 by www.worldwatch.org. Reproduced by permission.

We can be fairly confident now that major advertisers won't actually lie the way they did a century ago. Most of us have seen those antique medicine-bottle labels that claimed to cure everything from malaise to malaria, and we can laugh at how gullible people must have been then. But that may lull us into overlooking the newer ways advertisers have learned to manipulate us. Lies are only one kind of deception, perhaps the easiest kind to legislate against. But other kinds of dishonest messages are now all around us, in every medium—and I think getting worse. . . .

Advertising Affects Important Personal Decisions

Consider that advertising is now arguably the most pervasive and multifarious form of communication from which the modern public gets its beliefs about what makes life healthy, satisfying, and sustainable in the long run.

More people now get their impressions about what prescription medicines they need from magazine or TV ads than from their doctors. Notice all those ads for Claritan or Nexium or Lipitor, which largely drown out the advice of your doctor. It's you and your doctor who should be deciding what medicine you need, not you and a drug pusher. . . .

I'm fairly sure that more people decide what refrigerators, food, or clothes to buy because of the ads they've seen than because of evaluations they've gleaned from *Consumer Reports* or *Green Guide* or the Center for Science in the Public Interest.

FAST FACT

Four hours of television programming contain about one hundred advertisements.

Annual advertising expenditures in 2002 were about $247 billion in the United States alone. I doubt that the outreach budgets of public interest groups add up to one-tenth of 1 percent of that.

And, I'd bet that more people decide who to vote for as a result of direct advertising or other forms of paid persuasion than as a result of their appraisals of the candidates' policy papers or legislative track

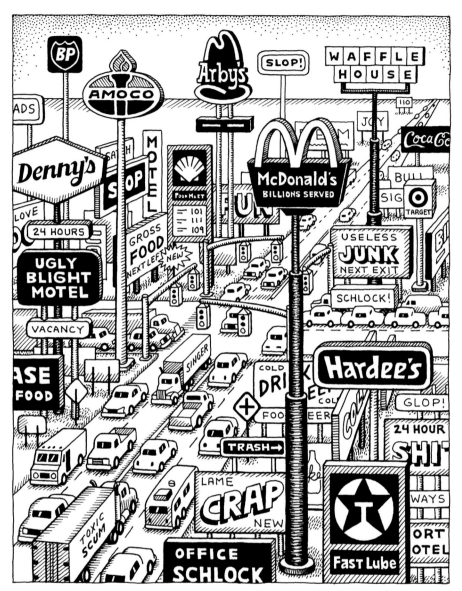

Andy Singer. Cagle Cartoons, Inc. Reproduced by permission.

records. Otherwise why does [President] G.W. Bush think he needs to raise $200 million for his reelection campaign, and why was [former presidential candidate] Howard Dean's early fundraising success considered so important? People will evidently learn more about these candidates from the ads they air than from what they've done with the governments of the United States or Vermont [where Dean was governor]. . . .

Sneaky Ads Manipulate Us

One way to see [how our perceptions are manipulated] is to recognize that perception is a form of physiological intake, just as is eating, drinking, or breathing. Like food, water, or air, the information we take in can be polluted. In the past few decades, the forms of pollution that have crept into our food, water, and air have proliferated—ranging from organic chemicals to invasive species to rogue genes from GMOs. And now, it seems, the various forms of information pollution, too, have proliferated. Advertising is transmogrifying into forms not always recognizable as advertising.

First, there's that seemingly innocuous form of industrial diplomacy known as public relations . . . at least since the 1930s, American businesses have been systematically—and very successfully—shaping public perceptions about everything from Coca-Cola to war.

Voters attend a political rally. Political advertising is critical to modern elections and can be very persuasive.

Drugs with Top Advertising Budgets

Drug	Condition	DTC Spending (in millions)	Sales (in billions)
Vioxx	Arthritis	$160.8	$1.5
Prilosec	Ulcer/reflux	107.5	4.1
Claritin	Allergy	99.7	2.0
Paxil	Anxiety/depression	91.8	1.8
Zocor	High cholesterol	91.2	2.2
Viagra	Impotence	89.5	0.8
Celebrex	Arthritis	78.3	2.0
Flonase	Allergy	73.5	0.6
Allegra	Allergy	67.0	1.1
Meridia	Obesity	65.0	0.1
Total		**$924.3**	**$16.3***

*Figures do not add up, due to rounding.

Source: National Institute of Health Care Management, "Prescription Drugs and Mass Media Advertising," www.nihcm.org, 2000.

Then, there's what we euphemistically call "product placement." For example, the movie *Chicago,* which won a lion's share of Oscars in 2002, contains numerous scenes (including the opening one) in which the camera moves in on a woman seductively smoking a brand of cigarette whose manufacturer has presumably paid a hefty fee to be so featured. . . .

Unable to Tell the Truth from an Ad

More recently, some advertisers have begun acquiring entire radio stations or publications of their own, in which they can pose as objective journalists. The National Rifle Association (NRA), for example, will soon be able to disseminate its anti-gun-control propaganda disguised as straight news.

Critics are concerned that the latter development will allow groups like the NRA to exploit free speech rules to avoid normal truth-in-advertising constraints, while ignoring the normal responsibilities of journalists. But an even bigger worry, I think, may be that as more and more media are aimed at manipulating consumer appetites or beliefs, using more and more sophisticated forms of disguise, the public will be increasingly unable to discriminate between responsible information services and propaganda and will gradually lose its freedom of independent thought and decision. If the ad comes disguised as a news report, scientific study, expert analysis, or neighbor's candid opinion, it may deceive even those who try to be vigilant. . . .

The Media Should Be Held Responsible for Restricting Ads

What might work now is for the media that carry advertising to be accountable for the claims of their advertisers. Traditionally, news media have maintained a "wall" between reporters and advertisers, ostensibly to protect reporters from conflicts of interest. But I suspect the real reason is that it allows publishers and editors (whose salaries are paid for by the ads) to distance themselves from any responsibility for the deceptions those ads perpetrate.

Now that the ads do at least as much to shape public worldviews, opinions, and lifestyles as does the reporting, however, it's time to stop that "see no evil" game the media play. Publishers, editors, and producers, as long as their papers or channels have not actually been bought up and taken over by their advertisers, should be the ones who hold those advertisers accountable. The *New Yorker*, which has courageously unmasked wrongdoing in U.S. policy and industry in many of its comment columns and articles, should now begin to unmask the hypocrisy of advertisers. It won't, of course, since it would likely not survive. But someday, perhaps, a publisher will do that—and will start a revolution in honest communications.

EVALUATING THE AUTHOR'S ARGUMENTS:

Ayres's main concern is that people will have difficulty telling the difference between factual news reports and advertisements that are meant to sell products. Why is Ayres concerned with this—what potential for danger does he see? Do you agree or disagree with him?

Some Advertising Should Not Be Restricted

Timothy R. Hawthorne

"Advertising changes minds, changes lives, even cultures and countries."

In the following viewpoint author Timothy R. Hawthorne argues that advertising should not be restricted because it improves our world. He points out that advertising in Africa has generated interest in products and services which have greatly enhanced the quality of life there. Advertising creates jobs and causes the economy to grow, he contends. Moreover, new technologies now enable people to skip advertisements if they so choose, making it unnecessary to put limits on advertising. He concludes that advertising enables our world to be more comfortable and creative and therefore should not be restricted.

Hawthorne is a chairman and executive creative director of an advertising agency. He has also worked as a television producer, writer, and director.

AS YOU READ, CONSIDER THE FOLLOWING QUESTIONS:

1. What changes occurred in Africa between 1970 and 2000 that Hawthorne uses to support his argument?

Timothy R. Hawthorne, "The Importance of Advertising," *Response,* vol. 13, January 2005, p. 46. Copyright © 2005 by Questex Media Group, Inc. All rights reserved. Reproduced by permission.

2. According to Hawthorne, what effect did advertising have on America in the 1920s and 1940s?
3. What percent of DVR users skip commercials, as reported by the author?

1970, Addis Ababa, Ethiopia:
I was teaching chemistry and physics to orphaned teens on the outskirts of this capital city. During the evenings, we'd watch the only two hours of broadcasting available—on a dilapidated black-and-white TV playing re-runs of *Dr. Who* from Britain. There were no commercials. JFK, Muhammad Ali and moon landings were all these kids knew about America. Kids and adults dressed in their traditional, floor length "gaabi" clothing wrap. There were few phones and no outdoor advertising except for the occasional Fanta soft drink or Biz soap signs. This was the Third World—a "primitive" world with few material possessions.

2000, Windhoek, Namibia:
My wife and I are producing a documentary on a worldwide volunteer teaching organization. In the evening, the blue glow of TVs can be seen in every home, whether tin shack or walled-in compound. Dozens of channels invade this starkly beautiful desert country. New acquaintances question us about "Florida's hanging chads" issue during the recent U.S. presidential election. Nikes, Adidas, Levis, even Lacoste labels can be seen everywhere. Traditional dress is non-existent, save the annual liberation day festivities. Billboards are everywhere. And everyone has a cell phone.

> **FAST FACT**
>
> According to author Peter Koeppel, viewers watch 20 to 30 percent more television once they get a personal video recorder, such as TiVo, but they use it to skip through 70 percent of the ads.

Advertising Powers Change

If anyone ever doubts the power of advertising—of mass media—they only need to visit modern day Africa. Though still rooted in a subsistence farming-based economy, Africa has been "globalized." And it is advertising that powered this change. For good or bad, advertising changes minds, changes lives, even cultures and countries.

How important is advertising to our economy? In late November, the Advertising Coalition—comprised of advertising giants like the Association of National Advertisers (ANA), the American Association of Advertising Agencies (AAAA) and the American Advertising Federation (AAF)—released a major new economic study for 2005 predicting $278 billion of company advertising will drive $5.2 trillion in sales and contribute to 21 million jobs. I believe the United States' unique approach to delivering advertising-supported mass media via radio (starting in the 1920s) and TV (premiering in the 1940s) enabled this country to experience unprecedented economic

People dance in a Namibian club. Some credit advertising with raising the standard of living in Third World countries such as Namibia.

The average child sees more than twenty thousand commercials a year. Some argue that advertising is simply part and parcel of American culture.

growth and innovation. Never before could companies deliver their selling message to so many people at one time. And no other country prospered so much and so quickly during the past 80 years.

Though Unpopular, Advertising Is an Important Part of Our World

For most of us, it's hard to imagine a world without advertising. We see more ads in one year than people 75 years ago saw in a lifetime. It's estimated we're exposed to between 250 and 1,000 advertising messages each day. And, according to the American Academy of Pediatrics, the average child sees more than 20,000 TV commercials a year.

It's all around us: our economy depends on it, yet most of the world detests advertising. Seventy-five percent of Europeans believe there is too much advertising. A . . . study reported more consumers have "wholly negative" feelings (36 percent) about advertising than "wholly positive" (28 percent). Sixty percent are more negative about advertising than they were a few years ago; and a whopping 69 percent want tools that block advertising completely. A world without advertising? Who could imagine such a place?

Viewers Have the Power to Skip Commercials

But the seed has been planted. Technology giveth the commercial and technology may taketh away. Last October [2004], Havas' Media Planning Group reported that 90 percent of DVR [digital video recorder] users always or usually skip commercials—with 57 percent saying they are simply annoyed by them. There will be 27 million DVRs in homes by 2008. Millions of commercials will never be seen. Unthinkable.

Madison Ave. is completely flummoxed. First, the proliferation of hundreds of channel options have made "mass advertising" nearly a thing of history. Strategically airing three TV spots was enough to reach 80 percent of women in 1965, but 97 spots are needed today. Now, viewers are taking control of whether they watch commercials or not.

Advertising Contributes to Our Economy and Culture

What does it all mean for the future of our economy and society? What impact would reducing our commercial ad intake from 500 to 50 a day have? Where do you stand on the importance of advertising?

Most likely, you're a part of this industry that fuels our economy and reflects and directs cultural changes. Next time you have a chance to vacation a couple of weeks away from all advertising, reflect on what impact our vocation has on our world. Would a world without advertising be less wealthy, less technological, less inventive, less comfortable?

EVALUATING THE AUTHORS' ARGUMENTS:

In this viewpoint Hawthorne argues that advertising has had positive effects on our society. In the previous viewpoint Ayres argues that advertising has had negative effects on our society. After reading both viewpoints, do you think advertising has more positive or more negative effects on society? Would you support or reject efforts to restrict it? Explain your answer.

Advertising Unfairly Targets Kids

Juliet B. Schor, interviewed by Lane Fisher

"It's remarkable that we have pretty much offered up our kids as a market to be exploited."

In this interview conducted by Lane Fisher, Juliet B. Schor argues that children are victims of advertising. Corporations care more about profit than about children's well-being, she claims, and engage in deceptive practices in order to sell their products. She describes how such techniques harm children by reducing their self-esteem and confusing their value systems. Schor concludes that parents, communities, and government must take action to curb advertising for the sake of America's youth.

Fisher is editor of *Hope* magazine. Schor, author of *Born to Buy*, is a professor of sociology at Boston College.

AS YOU READ, CONSIDER THE FOLLOWING QUESTIONS:

1. What is an example of "stealth marketing plans," as described by Schor?
2. Why does Schor believe that parents sometimes cooperate in what she considers advertisers' exploitation of their children?
3. According to Schor, what victory has been won over advertisers?

Lane Fisher, "Dematerializing Our Kids (an interview with Juliet B. Schor)," *Hope*, November/December 2004. Reproduced by permission of the author.

*L*ane Fisher: *What struck you most strongly about the ways corporations are cultivating children as consumers?*

Juliet Schor: That what's driving all this for corporations and advertisers is the bottom line, and there is a lot of denial about the impact of what they are doing on children's well-being. You see it most clearly with food products that are increasingly akin to alcohol and tobacco in that they are proving to be quite detrimental to kids' health. All the food advertising is for unhealthy foods—nobody is advertising broccoli—and junk food is a major factor in the obesity epidemic.

Advertisers Are Unethical

What I found is that there is virtually no space for advertisers to consider the ethics of what they are doing. The drive to succeed financially preempts any critical view of the product, even one like tobacco. With the exception of one company, which had a major anti-smoking account from the Legacy Foundation, I encountered no agency that said, "No, we won't take any tobacco money."

To me, it is really stunning that advertisers make so few ethical judgments about the products they take on. It is a monumental failure of social responsibility and conscience at the core of the advertising enterprise. It doesn't have to be that way. There is nothing inherent in advertising that says it can't have a good code of ethics.

A Captive Audience

LF: What do you consider some of the most unethical marketing practices you encountered?

JS: The whole gamut of in-school advertising is very problematic: captive audiences, an absence of parents, and a lot of advertising for junk food, violent movies, and violent video games. An estimated 40 percent of American middle- and high-schoolers watch Channel One every day of the academic year. The school signs a contract to show [news] programs with commercial advertising in return for a paltry gift of some video monitors without volume controls. So 40 percent of our kids are forced to view junk-food commercials. It is an outrage. . . .

Guerrilla Marketing

LF: Another marketing ploy that stunned me was peer marketing—paying college students to sit in bars and talk up a certain brand of alcohol, for instance. Why are marketers doing this, and how are they using younger children?

JS: Corporations understand the declining effectiveness of traditional television advertising—people now can zap the sound away or use gadgets that block out the commercials, plus there are so many ads that it makes it hard for one to stand out. On the grounds that word-of-mouth and personal endorsements are the most effective advertising they can buy, companies create what are called guerrilla, viral, or stealth marketing plans in which they enlist children. Sometimes they pay them, but more often they just give them free samples of the product and a set of instructions about how to spread the word about it. . . .

Opponents of advertising argue that the industry manipulates teens, who are unable to evaluate claims that advertisers make.

One company specializes in slumber parties for marketing. One girl will invite ten or eleven others over to watch a pilot for a TV show or try out a new product, sort of a focus group. Or they give a product to the other guests to try to get them to adopt it and pass it on to their other friends.

LF: You write that sometimes such slumber parties are videotaped. Why do parents allow that?

JS: You would be astonished at the extent to which people are accommodating the needs of marketers. People are allowing videotaping in virtually every aspect of their kids' lives. I think there are a few reasons for that, but it's partly how our sense of privacy has changed—we're accustomed to surveillance cameras all over the place. Then there's money, of course—people are getting paid—and this is especially attractive to the lower-income kids who are disproportionately targeted by marketers. But there also is a sense that this is how you get your fifteen minutes of fame. You're the star of a marketer's video. . . .

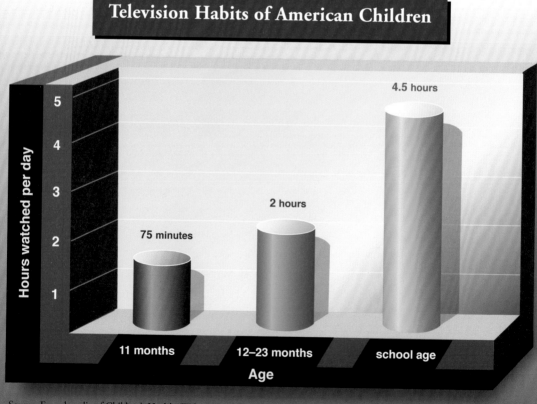

Television Habits of American Children

Source: Encyclopedia of Children's Health, "Television Habits," www.healthofchildren.com.

The Exploitation of Children

LF: How successful have parents been in countering these efforts?

JS: If you look at the big picture, the answer is, "Not." Under the influence of these marketers, kids' involvement in consumer culture has been growing over the last two decades and fairly dramatically in the last decade. It's remarkable that we have pretty much offered up our kids as a market to be exploited, with virtually no discussion, much less opposition.

But there are some victories. For example, Channel One got that 40 percent of schoolchildren as viewers pretty early on and, since then, has been unable to expand much. New York long ago passed a law against Channel One. So far the opposition to Channel One hasn't been able to dramatically reduce the fraction of kids who are watching it, but we may see a rollback. Seattle's school district has just voted it out. . . .

> **FAST FACT**
>
> According to a survey commissioned by the Center for a New American Dream, nearly a third of teenagers surveyed (32 percent) admit feeling pressure to buy certain products, such as clothes, shoes, and CDs, because their friends have them. Fifty-four percent of twelve- to thirteen-year-olds admit to feeling such pressure.

What Parents Can Do

LF: As a parent who has not allowed television in the home and has tried to hold a firm line, do you consider it the parent's job or the advertisers' responsibility to protect children?

JS: Well, I think it really lies in both places. Marketers are deliberately trying to make it very hard for parents to hold the line and be effective in their attempts to say "No." A lot of marketers' strategies—and I think they have figured out some very potent ones, especially for junk food—are designed to break down parental resistance.

My personal experience has been that I have had more ability to restrict than I would have thought, probably because of our television-free environment. Television is basically an advertising delivery system, especially for kids.

How Marketing Hurts Kids

LF: Until you did your own research on the impact of marketing to children, no one had shown that it is outright dangerous. What are some of the most important points you found in the two communities you studied?

JS: I looked at the overall impact of consumer culture on kids, as opposed to that of particular products, and what I found was that the kids that were more consumer involved became more depressed and anxious, had lower self-esteem, and were more likely to fight with their parents. I think this stems from the fact that they have adopted the sort of values, attitudes, and behaviors of consumer culture that turn out to undermine healthy psychological functioning. One of the marketers I interviewed said, "It is really harmful, what we are doing: we tell the kids that without our product, they are nothing, worthless." There is increasing research on adults to show that the more we compare ourselves with others, the more we worry about keeping up or about our status in the hierarchy, the worse off we are. What my research shows is that this mechanism is operating pretty powerfully with kids. . . .

What the Government Can Do

LF: In your book, you propose a national initiative to make outdoor space safe for children. Tell us how that plays into this picture.

JS: When kids are confined indoors, they are more likely to be using electronic media—television, video games, computers, videos, DVDs, et cetera, and these are all part of consumer culture. Kids love to play outdoors, and particularly on their own, but we have very large numbers of kids in this country who don't have a safe outdoor space.

LF: What are other actions you believe we must press Congress to take?

JS: I think a ban on food advertising is warranted at this point. Corporations would be very opposed to it, but it is a clean idea, much less complicated than saying, "You can't advertise a product if it has this fraction of sugar or this fraction of fat." Marketers need to be held ethically accountable for the ads they're making. We also need disclosure on most product placements [e.g., schools or celebrities paid to use a particular product] and a ban on in-school advertising—these are not on the immediate political horizon, obviously, but these are

Young adults are increasingly bombarded with commercialism wherever they go.

some of the kinds of things that I think would help us begin to get a handle on the problems. . . .

What Communities Can Do

LF: How can communities respond to the consumer culture's threat to kids?

JS: Creating awareness is a really good first step. Communities need to discuss these issues, most likely through schools, PTAs and PTOs, and so forth. Then, together, try to take steps that restrict children's consumer involvement. I interviewed parents who communicate with each other about which activities and products they might allow their children to be exposed to. That is really important, because that sets the peer context: if all the kids are restricted from something, it is not the same as a few of the kids being left out because their parents are stricter.

LF: What is the most important point in this for anyone who cares about children to understand?

JS: The consumer culture that we have created for kids is pernicious—it undermines their well-being—and we need to roll it back and give them a healthy culture to live in. And, by the way, the same is true for adults. If we can transform kids' consumer culture, we might actually create a much healthier, more life-affirming way of life for grown-ups, too.

EVALUATING THE AUTHOR'S ARGUMENTS:

Juliet B. Schor concludes that marketers exploit kids when they videotape them interacting with products. Do you agree or disagree with her assessment? Why or why not?

Advertising Does Not Unfairly Target Kids

Jacob Sullum

"While I have no doubt that advertising encourages children to request certain products, what happens after that is up to their parents."

In the following viewpoint Jacob Sullum argues that children are not targeted unfairly by advertisers. It is the responsibility of parents, and not corporations or regulatory laws, Sullum asserts, to protect kids. Sullum discusses recent lawsuit against the company Viacom, which has used cartoon characters to advertise unhealthy food to kids. The advertising is not unfair or illegal, Sullum contends, because the company has a right to sell its product. He concludes that parents are responsible for the ads their children see and the products they purchase for them.

Sullum is a syndicated newspaper columnist and senior editor of *Reason* magazine.

AS YOU READ, CONSIDER THE FOLLOWING QUESTIONS:
1. According to Sullum, how much does the Center for Science in the Public Interest (CSPI) believe parents should be entitled to in statutory damages each time a child sees an ad for unhealthy food?

Jacob Sullum, "Dora the Exploiter?" www.townhall.com, January 25, 2006. Copyright © 2006 by Creators Syndicate. Reproduced by permission of Creators Syndicate, Inc.

2. What does Sullum claim the CSPI ultimately wants to achieve?
3. What do you think the author means when he describes CSPI as a "nanny" group?

"Look!" exclaims my 3-year-old daughter, pointing excitedly at a box of cookies in the supermarket. "It's Dora! And Boots!" I nod and smile. "Yes, it is," I say, and we move on.

I do not feel injured by this exchange. But according to the Center for Science in the Public Interest (CSPI), a D.C.-based health nanny group, if I lived in Massachusetts the incident would be worth at least $25 in statutory damages.

Using that sort of reasoning, CSPI, the Boston-based Campaign for a Commercial-Free Childhood, and two Massachusetts parents who would rather sue multinational corporations than stand up to their own children are seeking billions of dollars in damages from Viacom (which owns Nickelodeon, home of *Dora the Explorer*) and Kellogg, maker of sugary breakfast cereals and other food products CSPI thinks your kids shouldn't eat. The plaintiffs say it's not about the money.

A Form of Censorship

I believe them. This lawsuit, which CSPI and its allies planto file under a Massachusetts consumer protection statute prohibiting "unfair or deceptive acts or practices," is really about censorship. By threatening onerous damages, CSPI aims to achieve through the courts what it has unsuccessfully demanded from legislators and regulators for decades: a ban on food advertising aimed at children.

The lawsuit argues that Viacom is on the hook for $25 "at a minimum" every time a kid in Massachusetts sees one of its characters attached to a "nutritionally poor" food product, or sees an ad for such a product on Nickelodeon or in another Viacom outlet. By CSPI's reckoning, Kellogg owes $25 whenever a child sees one of its ads, so an Apple Jacks commercial on Nickelodeon is worth $50 per viewer every time it airs.

"The injury continues . . . each time a parent purchases one of these items," says CSPI in a letter announcing its intent to sue. So if a parent, helpless to resist a preschooler's demands, actually buys the Dora cookies or the Apple Jacks, that's another $25 in damages. You can see how the bill starts to add up.

No Proof of Connection
But all the talk of injuries and damages is a charade. As obesity litigation advocate Richard Daynard notes in this month's *American Journal of Preventive Medicine,* one advantage of suing food companies under state consumer protection statutes is that it "avoids complicated causation issues."

Most of these laws "do not require a showing that the defendant's misbehavior caused a specific illness," writes Daynard, a Northeastern University law professor who plans to join CSPI in using such statutes to stop soda manufacturers from selling their products in schools.

Though advertisers do market their products to children, many argue it is their right to try and sell their product to customers.

Harley Schwadron. Reproduced by permission.

Indeed, "many state consumer protection statutes do not require a showing that individual plaintiffs relied on the [defendant's] misrepresentations."

Under the theory pressed by CSPI in its suit against Viacom and Kellogg, you don't even have to show that the companies misrepresented anything. CSPI argues that children "are intrinsically deceived and abused by encouragement to eat unhealthy junk foods," and it's seeking an injunction to stop all such encouragement.

The Responsibility of Parents

While I have no doubt that advertising encourages children to request certain products, what happens after that is up to their parents. Neither Viacom nor Kellogg has the power to dictate whether SpongeBob SquarePants Wild Bubble Berry Pop-Tarts are purchased, how often and in what quantities they're eaten, what else children eat or how much exercise they get.

"Nickelodeon and Kellogg engage in business practices that literally sicken our children," says CSPI Executive Director Michael Jacobson. Given the difficulty of demonstrating a causal connection between seeing Dora the Explorer on a box of cookies at age 3 and dying from obesity-related heart disease half a century later—precisely the difficulty CSPI is trying to avoid by filing this kind of suit—it would be more accurate to say these business practices figuratively sicken people like Michael Jacobson.

The question is how much weight the law should give to Jacobson's queasy gut.

EVALUATING THE AUTHORS' ARGUMENTS:

The previous viewpoint argues that companies should be responsible for protecting children from unfair advertising. Sullum argues that the responsibility lies solely with the parents. After reading both viewpoints, what do you think? Who should be responsible for protecting kids from unfair advertising?

Alcohol Advertising Causes Underage Drinking

Leslie B. Snyder et al.

"Youth reporting greater amounts of exposure to alcohol advertising ... drank more than youth who saw fewer ads."

In the following viewpoint Leslie B. Snyder and her colleagues argue that exposure to alcohol ads increases underage drinking. The authors conducted an extensive study that found that youth who saw more alcohol ads were more likely to drink. They were also more likely to increase their drinking levels over time. The authors conclude that more alcohol advertisements are aimed at youth than at adults, further increasing rates of underage drinking.

Snyder is a researcher in communication sciences at the University of Connecticut, as are the coauthors of the study.

AS YOU READ, CONSIDER THE FOLLOWING QUESTIONS:

1. According to the researchers, what percentage of drinks are consumed by underage drinkers?

2. What federal restrictions govern alcohol advertising?

3. According to the alcohol industry's code, what percentage of its advertisements must be aimed at adults?

T he causes of alcohol use among youth, including older children, adolescents, and young adults, are a major public health concern. Drinking among youth can result in a panoply of negative consequences, including poor grades, risky sex, alcohol addiction, and car crashes. Drinkers younger than 21 years, who consume approximately 20% of all alcoholic drinks, imbibe more heavily than adults per drinking episode and are involved in twice as many fatal car crashes while drinking. The problem is getting worse, with youth initiating drinking at an earlier age on average than they did in the past.

There is much public policy debate about whether alcohol advertising is partially responsible for youth consumption levels. The alcohol industry is not subject to federal restrictions on their advertising practices but has voluntary advertising codes created by the major alcohol trade groups. Even when the alcohol industry adheres to a code requiring that at least 70% of the audience (50% before fall 2003) for print, radio, and television advertisements consist of adults of legal drinking age, many youth are exposed to alcohol advertisements. There are often greater concentrations of alcohol advertisements in media aimed

FAST FACT

The Center for Media Education found that teens watch 100,000 alcohol commercials before they reach the legal drinking age.

at youth than at adults. However, studies of advertising content and youth exposure rates have not assessed the impact of advertising on youth. In 1997, the US Congress asked the National Institutes of Health for more scientific evidence on the relationship between advertising and alcohol use among those younger than the legal drinking age. . . .

Youth Are Affected by Alcohol Ads

We examined a national cohort of youth . . . to assess the effects of alcohol advertising on drinking amounts over time. The first hypothesis was that youth who reported greater exposure to alcohol advertising would have increased alcohol use over time. The second hypothesis concerned the effect of living in an environment with comparatively greater or fewer alcohol advertisements. By examining market-level measures of advertising expenditures per capita, we avoid the potential self-reporting bias among drinkers. We predicted that greater alcohol advertising expenditures per capita are correlated with greater youth drinking. . . .

The results of the present large-scale national . . . study provide evidence that the amount of advertising expenditures in 15- to 26-year-olds' media environment and the amount of advertising recalled related to greater youth drinking. Youth younger than the legal drinking age displayed a similar pattern of advertising effects as the entire age range, which is important because there is often a greater policy

A New Orleans police officer apprehends a teenager under the influence of alcohol. Some attribute America's teen drinking problem to alcohol advertising.

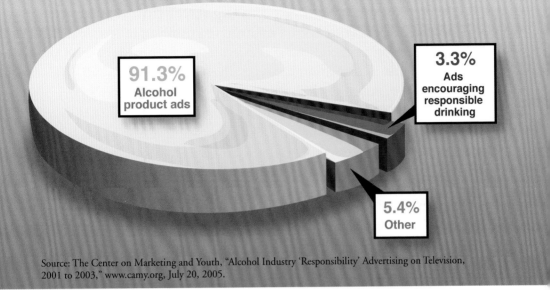

Alcohol Ads on Television

More than 90 percent of alcohol advertising dollars are spent on ads encouraging the purchase of alcohol, while less than 4 percent are spent on encouraging responsible drinking.

91.3%
Alcohol product ads

3.3%
Ads encouraging responsible drinking

5.4%
Other

Source: The Center on Marketing and Youth, "Alcohol Industry 'Responsibility' Advertising on Television, 2001 to 2003," www.camy.org, July 20, 2005.

interest in protecting underage youth from harmful communications than in protecting youth older than 21 years.

More Advertising Exposure Means More Drinking

Greater alcohol advertising expenditures in a market were related to both greater levels of youth drinking and steeper increases in drinking over time. Youth who lived in markets with more alcohol advertising drank more, increased their drinking levels more over time, and continued to increase drinking levels into their late 20s. Youth who lived in markets with less alcohol advertising drank less and showed a pattern of increasing their drinking modestly until their early 20s, when their drinking levels started to decline. The results are consistent with findings from studies of advertising bans and extend them by linking alcohol advertising expenditures per capita directly with individual youth behavior. . . .

The results are consistent with theories of cumulative effects of media exposure. Youth reporting greater amounts of exposure to alcohol advertising over the long term drank more than youth who saw fewer ads. Alcohol consumption was less sensitive to short-term differences in alcohol advertising exposure than to the long-term effects of exposure.

Commercial Watchers Are Paying Attention

Given that there was an impact on drinking using an objective measure of advertising expenditures, the results are inconsistent with the hypothesis that a correlation between advertising exposure and drinking could be caused entirely by selective attention on the part of drinkers. The results also contradict claims that advertising is unrelated to youth drinking amounts: that advertising at best causes brand switching, only affects those older than the legal drinking age, or is effectively countered by current educational efforts. Alcohol advertising was a contributing factor to youth drinking quantities over time.

> **EVALUATING THE AUTHORS' ARGUMENTS:**
>
> The authors of this viewpoint argue that alcohol advertising causes underage drinking. The authors of the next viewpoint disagree. After reading both viewpoints, which perspective do you agree with? Why? Support your answer with evidence from the text.

Alcohol Advertising Does Not Cause Underage Drinking

David J. Hanson

"Alcohol advertising doesn't increase overall consumption, doesn't contribute to alcohol abuse, and doesn't cause nondrinkers to become drinkers."

In the following viewpoint David J. Hanson argues that alcohol advertising does not cause underage drinking. He discusses hearings held by the New York state legislature on alcohol advertising, which aimed to determine whether such advertising has an effect on youth drinking. Hanson asserts that there is no scientific evidence demonstrating that advertisements encourage alcohol consumption or alcohol abuse by teenagers. Instead, alcohol advertising is only useful for convincing those who already drink to switch brands. He criticizes advocates of alcohol advertising bans for relying on what he calls junk science to support their arguments.

David J. Hanson is a sociology professor at the State University of New York at Potsdam and the author of *Alcohol Education: What We Must Do.*

AS YOU READ, CONSIDER THE FOLLOWING QUESTIONS:
1. What techniques did committee members use to express their arguments, and why were these unconvincing to Hanson?
2. What does the word *correlation* mean in the context of the viewpoint?
3. How do alcohol advertising critics misuse language, according to Hanson?

The New York State Assembly's Committee on Alcoholism and Drug Abuse held hearings [in 2002] on whether or not alcohol advertising has an effect on youthful drinking and, if so, what action the Assembly should take.

For most who testified, it was an article of faith: Alcohol ads causes young people to drink and strong action is needed. They converged on the hearing like the faithful assembling for a tent revival meeting. And their testimony was about as science-based as the rhetoric at a religious revival.

Ads Have No Bearing on Whether Youth Drink

Research from around the world has repeatedly demonstrated for decades that alcohol advertising doesn't increase overall consumption, doesn't contribute to alcohol abuse, and doesn't cause nondrinkers to become drinkers. However, what it has found is that successful advertisers increase their market share at the expense of their competitors, who lose market share.

But scientific evidence was irrelevant to the true believers, who showed great faith in their beliefs. As one testified, "we should trust our eyes and ears" instead of believing what science has demonstrated.

Because those who opposed alcohol advertising were not supported by the scientific facts, they were forced to rely on anecdotal stories, emotional appeals, impressions, beliefs, and extensive use of "junk science." Of course there were testimonials, without which no tent meeting would be complete.

Meaningless Correlations Between Ads and Underage Drinking

To "prove" that alcohol ads cause young people to drink, the faithful resorted to polls indicating that many people *think* alcohol ads increase youthful drinking. But polls also find that many people *think* that extraterrestrial aliens have landed on earth, that ghosts can communicate with us, and that some races are systematically inferior to others.

The true believers made great use of correlations that never, even once, proved anything. We know that increased consumption of ice cream is correlated with an increase in drownings. But that doesn't mean that eating ice cream causes people to drown. People are more likely to both eat ice cream and to go swimming (and sometimes drown) in warm weather.

Many reject the suggestion that alcohol advertisements, such as this Budweiser ad, have any impact on underage drinking.

Research has shown that alcohol advertisements do not encourage people to drink, but rather encourage those who already drink to switch brands.

Virtually every true believer used meaningless correlations to convince legislators to impose additional restrictions on advertising. Reflecting either naiveté or contempt for the Constitutionally guaranteed First Amendment free-speech rights of others, some even called for the prohibition of alcohol advertising.

Misusing Language

The junk science congregation tended to have its own vocabulary, with meanings different from the "outside world." For example, much was made of alcohol ads appearing in youth-oriented magazines. To most people a youth-oriented magazine would have at least a majority of youthful readers. But to be clearly youth-oriented, perhaps the readership should be two-thirds young people, or perhaps three-fourths. Would you believe that anything above 15.8% youthful readership was defined as a youth-oriented magazine?!

This definition may be counter-intuitive, but if a common-sense definition were used the "researchers" wouldn't have any headline-grabbing findings to report. That's the nature of junk science. Those who practice it are interested in sound bites instead of sound science.

The misuse of language to persuade was pervasive. For example, believers defined the term "binge" so loosely that a so-called binge drinker needn't have any measurable blood alcohol concentration (BAC). Similarly, 20-year-old married adults serving their country in the military would be "kids." Persuading others rather than presenting facts accurately is the goal of junk science.

Rely on Facts, Not Fervor and Zeal

The true believers had faith, deep conviction, emotional fervor and proselytizing zeal. What they didn't have was a shred of scientific evidence to support any of their beliefs and recommendations.

A the end of the day, the faithful returned home to the Center for Addiction and Substance Abuse, the Center for Science in the Public Interest, the Center on Alcohol Marketing and Youth, and other bastions of committed believers to refresh their zeal.

EVALUATING THE AUTHOR'S ARGUMENTS:

To make his argument that alcohol advertisements are not responsible for underage drinking, David J. Hanson calls those who oppose him as "true believers" and described them as being zealous and filled with "emotional fervor." How did these descriptions affect your reading of his argument? Did such language help persuade you of his point, or not? Explain your answer.

Junk Food Advertising Is to Blame for Childhood Obesity

Ted Lempert

"The role of marketing in the childhood obesity problem is significant."

In the following viewpoint Ted Lempert argues that advertising is responsible for the growing obesity rates of American children. Lempert suggests that exposure to advertising directly influences children's food preferences and requests. Children who watch more advertising for junk food, he claims, are more likely to consume junk food. Manufacturers take advantage of kids by disguising advertisements in television shows, video games, or toys, says Lempert. Because children do not understand the intent of advertisements, Lempert suggests that advertising in children's programming should be restricted.

Lempert is the president of the organization Children Now, a national children's advocacy organization.

1. According to the author, how much has the obesity rate increased in the past three decades?
2. How many television commercials does Lempert claim that the average child sees annually?
3. At what age does Lempert contend children can begin to be influenced in regard to brand preferences?

For the first time in modern history, our children's life expectancy could be lower than our own. The reason: obesity. In the past three decades, there has been a 300 percent increase in the rate of U.S. children who are either overweight or obese, according to the National Center for Health Statistics. Although one can point to several reasons for this crisis, one culprit is the commercialism to which children are exposed every day. Like the obesity crisis, this commercialism will only increase if steps are not taken to stem it now.

Young People See Thousands of Ads

Every day our children are bombarded with advertisements—quite often for products that are harmful to them. Each year, the average child sees about 40,000 commercials on television alone, according to communications professor Dale Kunkel of the University of Arizona; the majority of ads targeted at them are for candy, sugared cereal, soda and fast food.

While parents may actually be the ones paying the price for all of this advertising at the cash register, our children are paying with their health. In addition to the social stigma and psychological effects that overweight children often suffer, they are also significantly more likely than their peers to become afflicted with serious health problems such as asthma, diabetes, high blood pressure and sleep apnea. In fact, the U.S. Surgeon General has identified overweight and obesity as "the fastest growing cause of disease and death in America."

Preying on Children

The role of marketing in the childhood obesity problem is significant. A recent Stanford study found that children who spend the most time

Childhood obesity is a growing problem in America, one which many attribute to the abundance of junk food products and advertising.

watching TV, videos and video games are more likely to be overweight. A 1999 study in the *Journal of the American Medical Association* also shows that exposure to food commercials influences children's food preferences and requests.

The pervasiveness of marketing to children is particularly troubling because of kids' inherent vulnerability to persuasion. Children under age 8 do not recognize the intent of ads and tend to accept them as accurate and unbiased. A 30-second commercial can influence brand preferences in children as young as 2, Kunkel has found.

Many advertisers prey upon children's vulnerability by disguising their advertisements as online games or by using product placement to sneak them into prime-time shows. It is through television, computers and video games that perhaps the most insidious attempts to manipulate children's eating habits occur. It is where food advertisers spend billions of dollars each year pushing unhealthy cereals, snacks and drinks through commercials and product placements aimed at children; where beloved cartoon characters shill for fast-food chains (such as Burger King's use of Teletubbies and SpongeBob); and where advertisements for cookies and candy are disguised as arcade-style games. It is where broadcasters and advertisers put their own financial well-being above the health of our children.

A Responsibility to Do Better

The media and advertisers have a responsibility to do better by our nation's kids. Some have recognized the effects their business practices have on children and are taking important steps toward acting

Andy Singer. Cagle Cartoons, Inc. Reproduced by permission.

Opponents of advertising believe soft drink machines should be removed from schools to prevent childhood obesity.

in children's best interest. In January [of 2005], Kraft Foods decided to stop advertising its low-nutrition foods during children's programs and replace them with ads for more nutritional snack products. *Sesame Street* recently teamed with Earth's Best to launch a new line of organic and "nutrient-rich" breakfast foods and snacks for children. Nickelodeon refused to allow one of its characters, Dora the Explorer, to be used for a Burger King kids' meal unless a piece of fruit was included in the meal.

These are all important steps toward improving the nutritional messages children receive from the media. Other broadcasters and advertisers need to follow suit and develop business practices that will support, rather than thwart, children's healthy development. For instance, they can dedicate a certain percentage of advertising time to pro-nutrition public-service announcements. And if broadcasters are going to license their characters, these characters can sell healthy foods.

The Future of Advertising

Yet more must be done to protect our nation's children, especially in a rapidly changing technological era. Digital, interactive television is on the horizon, and it promises to change the way companies push their marketing on children. Imagine watching a television show that has logos for McDonald's, Snickers, Jell-o Pudding, and the new "American Pie 6" movie scattered about the bottom of the screen. Imagine that you or your children could click on those logos with your remote control and be instantly transported to Web sites for those products where your child could purchase items from those sites directly from your TV.

Interactive television also has the potential to target individual viewers with personalized ads, increasing the likelihood of impulse purchases, according to the Center for Digital Democracy. Advertisers will be able to target children according to their gender, age, household income and race, by tracking the history of their individual television viewing habits.

The Federal Communications Commission must intervene now to ensure that children are protected from interactive advertising before it ever has a chance to become a common marketing technique. . . . It is essential that the commission move forward and prohibit this practice to protect our nation's kids.

EVALUATING THE AUTHOR'S ARGUMENTS:

In this viewpoint Lempert discusses product placement and claims it is particularly harmful. What is product placement? Do you agree or disagree that it is harmful? Explain your reasoning.

Viewpoint

8

Junk Food Advertising Is Not to Blame for Childhood Obesity

"Parents, not food advertising, represent the primary factor in kids' food choices and weight."

Richard Berman

In the following viewpoint Richard Berman argues that advertising does not contribute to childhood obesity. While food corporations are often blamed for their aggressive advertising to youth, Berman cites studies showing that junk food ads do not cause kids to gain weight or eat unhealthy foods. Americans have become more sedentary than in previous generations, and Berman claims that children's rising weights are simply the result of not working off as many calories as they consume.

Berman is executive director of the Center for Consumer Freedom, a nonprofit coalition of restaurants, food companies, and consumers.

AS YOU READ, CONSIDER THE FOLLOWING QUESTIONS:

1. According to Berman's sources, what effect has banning food advertising to children had in Sweden and Quebec?

2. How does the author explain the connection between television watching and childhood obesity?
3. According to Berman, what percentage of American teenagers participate in weekly physical education classes at school?

Everywhere you look, food advertising is being blamed for childhood obesity. The World Health Organization and the Institute of Medicine have hit the industry for its practices. The Federal Trade Commission is getting in the game. And in recent weeks Iowa Sen. Tom Harkin has threatened advertisers and food companies with draconian legislation.

Harkin's statements invoke a body of scientific evidence supposedly linking food advertising with childhood obesity. To put it nicely, this is wishful thinking. There is simply no solid evidence of a connection. At the same time, there are many compelling reasons to believe that no relationship exists.

No Link Between Advertising and Obesity

The vast majority of people believe that parents, not food advertising, represent the primary factor in kids' food choices and weight. And the experts agree. "Despite media claims to the contrary," one recent article in *The Journal of the Royal Society of Medicine* noted, "there is no good evidence that advertising has a sub-

stantial influence on children's food consumption and, consequently, no reason to believe that a complete ban on advertising would have any useful impact on childhood obesity rates." The article pointed out that countries such as Sweden, and provinces such as Canada's Quebec, have banned food advertising to kids, and they're no thinner than the rest of us.

Even the inventor of punitive "fat taxes" (also known as the "Twinkie tax"), Yale University Professor Kelly Brownell admits: "There is only circumstantial evidence that the ads cause poor eating." The "circumstantial" evidence generally cited by anti-advertising crusaders relates to a moderate correlation between TV viewing and childhood obesity. Of course, the fact that watching TV is a sedentary behavior in itself is rarely mentioned. Nor do industry opponents like to admit that the connection between obesity and video games (where food advertising is rare) is much stronger than the connection between obesity and TV viewing.

Lack of Activity Causes Obesity

It's easy for politicians to blame food advertising. That's because regulating it doesn't cost any money. But the true driver of childhood obesity these days is a steady decline in physical activity—and addressing that problem will require serious tradeoffs.

Many blame childhood obesity on the fact that American children do not get enough exercise, rather than on junk food advertising.

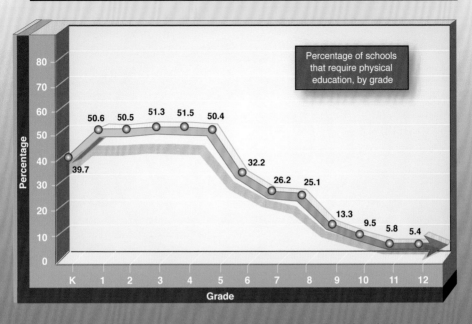

Students Get Less Physical Education as They Age

Percentage of schools that require physical education, by grade

39.7 50.6 50.5 51.3 51.5 50.4 32.2 26.2 25.1 13.3 9.5 5.8 5.4

Percentage

Grade

Source: CDC's School Health Policies and Programs Study (SHPPS), "Fact Sheet: Physical Education and Activity," www.cdc.gov/HealthyYouth/shpps.

"In a debate that has often focused on foods alone," former Food and Drug Commissioner Dr. Mark McClellan observes, "actual levels of caloric intake among the young haven't appreciably changed over the last 20 years." Unlike Mr. Harkin's claims about food advertising, a growing body of research does indeed corroborate McClellan's point.

Earlier this year, research published in the Archives of Pediatrics and Adolescent Medicine found "insufficient vigorous physical activity was the only risk factor" for overweight children. An article in *The American Journal of Clinical Nutrition* noted: "The lack of evidence of a general increase in energy intake among youths despite an increase in the prevalence of overweight suggests that physical inactivity is a major public health challenge in this age group." And an article in *The Journal of Clinical Endocrinology & Metabolism* pointed out: "It is often assumed that the increase in pediatric obesity has occurred because of an increase in caloric intake. However, the data do not substantiate this."

All of this makes intuitive sense. If Grandpa hiked three miles in the snow (uphill both ways, of course) to get to school, and Dad traveled to junior high on his bike, today's kids get door-to-door service

A student learns about correct portion size. Teaching American children better eating habits could reduce the problem of childhood obesity.

in the family minivan. Walking and biking trips made by children have dropped more than 60% since the late 1970s. A full quarter of American children get no physical activity whatsoever.

Schools have become part of the problem. With tight budgets and a renewed focus on reading and math, gym is going the way of the dinosaurs. An article in the journal *Pediatrics* found that only 21% of American adolescents participate in a physical education class each week.

Food and Advertising Are Not to Blame

Meanwhile, food is getting a bum rap. It may sound counterintuitive, but after studying more than 14,000 American children, a team of six Harvard doctors found that snack food and soda do not contribute to childhood obesity. The study, which was published in *The International Journal of Obesity,* concluded: "Our data did not offer support for the hypothesis that snacking promotes weight gain."

As is often the case in emotionally charged debates, policy is getting far ahead of research. The self-described "food police" at the Center for Science in the Public Interest have urged litigation by trial lawyers and state attorneys general to restrict food advertising to children. A government commission in Maine recently proposed extra taxes on advertising certain foods to kids. And-*sacre bleu!*—France has already enacted such a proposal.

The science may not be on their side, but industry opponents have the momentum. Defending food advertising in this environment has certain risks. Nevertheless, the risks associated with giving in to political pressure are even greater. . . .

Whether in the courtroom, or the court of public opinion, voluntarily limiting food advertising to children looks like an implicit admission of guilt. . . . Better to spend more money promoting the real evidence rather than making concessions to those who will continuously and incrementally move the goalposts.

> ### EVALUATING THE AUTHORS' ARGUMENTS:
>
> In this viewpoint Berman argues that junk food advertising has no affect on childhood obesity. In the previous viewpoint Lempert argues that advertising causes childhood obesity. After reading both viewpoints, which argument do you agree with? Why?

Facts About Advertising

Editor's note: These facts can be used in reports or papers to reinforce or add credibility when making important points or claims.

Advertising Firsts
- The first American magazine ads appeared in Benjamin Franklin's *General* Magazine in 1742.
- The first advertising agency was opened in Philadelphia in 1843.
- The first convention of advertising agents was held in New York in 1873.
- In 1938 radio overtook newspapers as a source of advertising revenue.
- The first television ad for a political candidate aired in 1950. It was for Senator William Benton of Connecticut.
- In 1954 CBS became the largest advertising medium in the world.
- Dwight D. Eisenhower's 1956 campaign was the first presidential race which relied heavily on television commercials.
- Cigarette ads were first banned from magazines in 1964.
- In 1976 the Supreme Court granted advertising protection under the First Amendment.

Advertising Spending
According to TNS Media Intelligence, advertisers spent a total of $143.3 billion pushing their products via the U.S. media in 2005. They spent:

> $25.1 billon advertising in newspapers
> $22.4 billion advertising on network television
> $15.9 billion advertising on cable television
> $21.7 billion advertising in consumer magazines
> $8.3 billion advertising on the Internet
> $7.4 billion advertising on local radio
> $4.5 billion advertising in business-to-business magazines
> $1 billion advertising on network radio

- Thirty seconds of advertising during the Super Bowl costs $2.4 million.
- U.S. spending on online local advertising is expected to grow 26 percent to $3.2 billion in 2005. Online advertising is expected to reach $5.3 billion by 2010.

- Product placement inside video games is expected to reach $260 million by 2008, up from $79 million in 2003.

Advertising and Children
- According to a 2004 survey by the Kaiser Family Foundation, half (49 percent) of parents say children's food choices and eating habits are influenced "a lot" by food advertising on TV, and a third (33 percent) say their children "often" ask them to buy things at the grocery store that they have seen in TV ads.

According to the National Institute on Media and the Family:
- The average American child may view as many as forty thousand television commercials every year.
- Children as young as age three recognize brand logos, with brand loyalty influence starting at age two.
- Young children are not able to distinguish between commercials and TV programs. They do not recognize that commercials are trying to sell something.
- Children who watch a lot of television want more toys seen in advertisements and eat more advertised food than children who do not watch as much television.
- Four hours of television programming contain about one hundred ads.

According to the organization New American Dream:
- An estimated $13 billion a year is spent marketing to American children by food and drink industries alone. Food advertising makes up about half of all advertising aimed at kids.
- At three years of age, before they can read, one out of five American children is already making specific requests for brand-name products.

Advertising and Alcohol
- The Center for Science in the Public Interest found that the beer-brewing industry alone spent more than $770 million on television ads and $15 million on radio ads in 2000.

According to the American Academy of Pediatrics:
- American children view two thousand beer and wine commercials per year.

- Fifty-six percent of students in grades five through twelve say that alcohol advertising encourages them to drink.

According to the Federal Trade Commission:
- Alcohol companies placed their product in 233 motion pictures and in one or more episodes of 181 different television series in 1997–1998. In the 15 shows most popular with teens, 8 had alcohol product placements.
- Alcohol placement has occurred in PG and PG 13 movies where the primary audience included a sizable number of teens and children.
- Alcoholic-beverage companies have created over a hundred Web sites to advertise and promote their products. Many of those sites have a strong appeal to youth and can include interactive games and contests.

Advertising and the Law
- The Federal Trade Commission (FTC) is the primary regulator of deceptive advertising in the United States. It was created in 1914.

According to the University of Texas at Austin, Department of Advertising:
Commercial speech can be regulated if:
- it is misleading or concerns an illegal product, or if
- there is a substantial government interest, and
- the regulation directly advances that government interest, and
- the regulation is narrowly tailored to that interest.

Perceptions of Advertising
An April 2004 Yankelovich Partners poll for the American Association of Advertising Agencies found that of the Americans they surveyed:
- 65 percent said they believed that they "are constantly bombarded with too much" advertising;
- 61 percent agreed that the amount of advertising and marketing to which they are exposed "is out of control";
- 60 percent said their opinion of advertising "is much more negative than just a few years ago";
- 54 percent of the survey respondents said they "avoid buying products that overwhelm them with advertising and marketing";
- 69 percent said they "are interested in products and services that would help them skip or block marketing."

Adbusters Media Foundation

1234 West 7th Ave.
Vancouver, BC V6H 1B7
(604) 736-9401
e-mail: info@adbusters.org
Web site: www.adbusters.org

Adbusters is a network of artists, activists, writers, and other people who oppose rampant commercialism. The organization publishes *Adbusters* magazine, which explores the ways that commercialism destroys physical and cultural environments. Spoof ads and information on political action are available on the organization's Web site.

Ad Council

261 Madison Ave., 11th Floor
New York, NY 10016
(212) 922-1500
e-mail: info@adcouncil.org
Web site: www.adcouncil.org

The Ad Council is a nonprofit organization that works with businesses, advertisers, the media, and other nonprofit groups to produce and distribute public service campaigns.

Advertising Standards Canada (ASC)

175 Bloor St. E., South Tower, Suite 1801
Toronto, ON M4W 3R8
(416) 961-6311
e-mail: info@adstandards.com
Web site: www.adstandards.com

Advertising Standards Canada is an organization that has more than 170 corporate members, including advertising agencies and media. ASC promotes the use of industry self-regulation as a way to ensure the integrity of advertising.

Alliance for Better Campaigns
1990 M St. NW, Suite 200
Washington, DC 20036
(202) 659-1300
e-mail: alliance@bettercampaigns.org
Web site: www.bettercampaigns.org

The Alliance for Better Campaigns is a public interest group whose goal is to improve elections by reforming political campaigns. The alliance believes that these reforms, which include reducing the cost of political communication and requiring broadcasters to provide better coverage of political issues, will increase political competition and make voters more informed.

Association of National Advertisers (ANA)
708 Third Ave.
New York, NY 10017-4270
(212) 697-5950
Web site: www.ana.net

The Association of National Advertisers is a trade association that offers resources and training to the advertising industry. Its members provide services and products to more than three hundred companies that combined spend over $100 billion on advertising and marketing. The association publishes the magazine *Advertiser* six times each year.

Campaign Legal Center
1640 Rhode Island Ave. NW, Suite 650
Washington, DC 20036
(202) 736-2200
e-mail: info@campaignlegalcenter.org
Web site: www.campaignlegalcenter.org

The Campaign Legal Center is a nonprofit and nonpartisan organization that represents the public interest in issues relating to campaign finance and associated media laws. The center also develops legal and policy debate on political advertising.

Center for a New American Dream
6930 Carroll Ave., Suite 900
Takoma Park, MD 20912
(301) 891-3683

(877) 68-DREAM

e-mail: newdream@newdream.org

Web site: www.newdream.org

The Center for a New American Dream is an organization whose goal is to help Americans consume responsibly by protecting the earth's resources. Its *Kids and Commercialism* campaign provides information on the effects of advertising on children.

Center on Alcohol Marketing and Youth (CAMY)

2233 Wisconsin Ave. NW, Suite 525

Washington, DC 20007

(202) 687-1019

e-mail: info@camy.org

Web site: camy.org

Based at Georgetown University, the Center on Alcohol Marketing and Youth focuses attention on the marketing practices of the alcohol industry, in particular those that may cause harm to America's youth. The Web site features numerous reports and fact sheets on alcohol advertising and the consequences of underage drinking, including *Clicking with Kids: Alcohol Marketing and Youth on the Internet* and *Overexposed: Youth a Target of Alcohol Advertising in Magazines.*

Children's Advertising Review Unit (CARU)

70 West 36th St., 13th Floor

New York, NY 10018

(866) 334-6272 (ext.111)

e-mail: caru@caru.bbb.org

Web site: www.caru.org

As the children's branch of the U.S. advertising industry's self-regulation program, the Children's Advertising Review Unit reviews ads aimed at children and promotes responsible children's advertising. It also corrects misleading or inaccurate commercials with the help of advertisers.

Commercial Alert

4110 SE Hawthorne Blvd., #123

Portland, OR 97214

(503) 235-8012

e-mail: info@commercialalert.org

Web site: www.commercialalert.org

Commercial Alert is a nonprofit organization whose goal is to prevent commercial culture from exploiting children and destroying family and community values. It works toward that goal by conducting campaigns against commercialism in classrooms and marketing to children.

Commercialism in Education Research Unit (CERU)
Box 872411, Arizona State University
Tempe, AZ 85287-2411
(480) 965-1886
e-mail: ceru@asu.edu
Web site: www.asu.edu/educ/epsl/ceru.htm

The Commercialism in Education Research Unit conducts research and distributes information about commercial activities in schools.

Federal Trade Commission–Bureau of Consumer Protection
600 Pennsylvania Ave. NW
Washington, DC 20580
(202) 326-2222
Web site: www.ftc.gov/ftc/consumer/home.html

Part of the Federal Trade Commission, the Bureau of Consumer Protection defends consumers against fraudulent or destructive practices. The Bureau's Division of Advertising Practices protects people from deceptive advertising by monitoring advertisements for numerous products, including tobacco, alcohol, and over-the-counter drugs.

Media Awareness Network
1500 Merivale Rd., 3rd Floor
Ottawa, ON K2E 6Z5
(613) 224-7721
e-mail: info@media-awareness.ca
Web site: www.media-awareness.ca

The Media Awareness Network is a nonprofit organization that promotes media education and develops media literacy programs. Its Media Issues section examines topics such as marketing to children and stereotyping in advertisements. The Web site also provides information for parents and educators.

Books

Acuff, Daniel, and Robert Reiher, *Kidnapped: How Irresponsible Marketers Are Stealing the Minds of Your Children*. Chicago: Dearborn, 2005. The authors, marketing researchers and consultants, discuss the impact of media exposure on children and how child development plays into advertising techniques.

Cortese, Anthony J., *Provocateur: Images of Women and Minorities in Advertising*. New York: Rowman and Littlefield, 2004. Offers analysis of images of women and minorities in advertising and argues that contrary to popular opinion, sex and violence do not always sell.

Garfield, Bob, *And Now a Few Words from Me: Advertising's Leading Critic Lays Down the Law, Once and for All*. Chicago: Contemporary Books, 2003. *Advertising Age* columnist Garfield lampoons unsuccessful advertisements and lays out standards for what makes a good advertisement.

Gudis, Catherine, *Buyways: Automobility, Billboards, and the American Cultural Landscape*. New York: Routledge, 2004. Describes how the automobile has turned the landscape into a site of commerce, tracing the history of outdoor advertising in America.

Kitch, Carolyn, *The Girl on the Magazine Cover: The Origins of Visual Stereotypes in American Mass Media*. Chapel Hill: University of North Carolina Press, 2001. A history of how American women's magazines have marketed a conventional model of womanhood and how editorial and advertising messages have been blurred.

Linn, Susan E., *Consuming Kids: The Hostile Takeover of Childhood*. New York: New Press, 2004. Explains how advertising targets kids, from "prenatal marketing" to teenagers. Argues that successful advertising often exploits children and that the advertising industry wields a dangerous degree of power.

Quart, Alissa, *Branded: The Buying and Selling of Teenagers*. New York: Basic Books, 2003. Explores how teenagers are targeted by marketers, delving into such subjects as cosmetic surgery, video game obsessions, and "name-brand" colleges.

Ries, Al, *The Fall of Advertising and the Rise of PR*. New York: HarperBusiness, 2002. Argues that advertising has become more of a creative art than a selling tool.

Samuel, Lawrence R., *Brought to You By: Postwar Television Advertising and the American Dream*. Austin: University of Texas Press, 2002. A history of how advertising became one of the shaping forces of American culture after World War II.

Schor, Juliet, *Born to Buy: The Commercialized Child and the New Consumer Culture*. New York: Scribner, 2004. Details how advertising targets kids and what parents, educators, and advertisers can do to fix this problem.

Spence, Edward, Brett Van Heekeren, and Michael Boylan, *Advertising Ethics*. New York: Prentice Hall, 2004. An evaluation of the ethical issues that arise in advertising, including case studies and the relationship of advertising to the community.

Twitchell, James B., *Twenty Ads That Shook the World: The Century's Most Groundbreaking Advertising and How It Changed Us All*. New York: Crown, 2000. A history of twenty of the most influential advertisements of the twentieth century and how they affected American culture.

Zyman, Sergio, *The End of Marketing as We Know It*. New York: John Wiley and Sons, 2002. The former chief marketing officer for Coca-Cola uses real world examples to show what makes an effective advertisement and what does not.

Periodicals

Fass, Allison, "Advertising on Demand," *Forbes*, July 25, 2005.

Harder, Ben, "Pushing Drugs: How Medical Marketing Influences Doctors and Patients," *Science News*, July 30, 2005.

Jeffers, Michelle, "Behind Dove's 'Real Beauty': Why Ogilvy Decided to Ditch the Size 2 Models," *ADWEEK*, Sept 12, 2005.

Kelly, Katy, and Linda Kulman, "Kid Power," *U.S News & World Report*, September 13, 2004.

Kennedy, David G., "Coming of Age in Consumerdom," *American Demographics,* April 1, 2004.

Kiley, David, "Laughing Out Loud in Spanish: Warm-and-Fuzzy Hispanic TV Ads Are Giving Way to the Crude and Funny," *Business Week,* March 20, 2006.

Marketing Week, "Is Product Placement Commercial Salvation?" March 17, 2005.

Meier, Christian, "Ads Becoming More Creative, Less Orthodox," *Philadelphia Inquirer,* August 28, 2005.

Melillo, Wendy, "Bringing Up Baby: Where's the Line, and Who Should Draw It, in Advertising to Children?" *ADWEEK,* February 13, 2006.

Nelson, Jon P., "Alcohol, Advertising, and Youth: Is the Alcoholic Beverage Industry Targeting Minors with Magazine Ads?" *Regulation,* Summer 2005.

Obermiller, Carl, Eric Spangenberg, and Douglas L. MacLachlan, "Ad Skepticism: The Consequences of Disbelief," *Journal of Advertising,* Fall 2005.

Parry, Caroline, "Is Advertising Proving Irresistible?" *Marketing Week,* July 8, 2004.

Pollack, Judann, "A Few Real Women Weigh In: Dove Ads Kick Nike's Big Butt," *Advertising Age,* August 22, 2005.

Ralston, Richard E., "Adding Value, Lowering Drug Costs—with Advertising," *San Francisco Gate,* June 22, 2005.

Sachs, Andrea, "Junk Culture: Author Juliet Schor Explores How Marketing Has Invaded Childhood," *Time,* October 4, 2004.

Sennott, Sara, "Customer Placement; the Latest Marketing Trend Makes the Consumer a Player Inside the Commercial," *Newsweek International,* November 29, 2004.

Stone, Brad, "New Ways to Drive Home the Message," *Newsweek,* May 30, 2005.

Till, Brian D., and Daniel W. Baack, "Recall and Persuasion: Does Creative Advertising Matter?" *Journal of Advertising,* Fall 2005.

Washington Post, "Viewer Beware," April 24, 2005.

Wood, Daniel B., "Has Hidden Advertising Gone Too Far?" *Christian Science Monitor*, November 17, 2005.

Web Sites

Ad Flip (www.adflip.com). A searchable database of classic print ads from the 1940s through 2000.

Gender Ads (www.genderads.com). A resource for analyzing advertising images that relate to gender, dealing with topics such as marriage, violence, and homosexuality.

Online Communication Studies Resources (www.uiowa.edu/~commstud/resources/advertising.html). The University of Iowa Department of Communication Studies' site, with links to information about advertising history, law, ethics, and other areas of interest.

Texas Advertising (http://advertising.utexas.edu/research/law). The University of Texas at Austin Department of Advertising manages this site on advertising law and ethics.

The :30 Second Candidate (www.pbs.org/30secondcandidate/front.html). From Public Broadcasting Service, a look at the world of political advertising, its history, and how it works.

Index

Supreme Court, 16

television, 52
  alcohol commercials on,
    67–69
  children and, 28, 78
  product placement on, 20,
    25–26

Vaccaro, Brenda, 23

Voight, Joan, 34

Wall Street Journal
  (newspaper), 22, 23

Young, Neil, 24
youth, 57
  alcohol ads and, 67–69,
    72–74
  see also children

Picture Credits

Cover: Mitchell Funk/Getty Images
Maury Aaseng, 20, 30, 46, 56, 69, 85
AP/Wide World Photos, 11, 13, 18, 24, 25, 41, 50, 73, 80, 86
Monty Brinton/CBS/Landov, 32
© Everett Kennedy Brown/epa/CORBIS, 74
© Radhika Chalasani/CORBIS, 78, 84
© Ole Graf/zefa/CORBIS, 55
Lucas Jackson/Reuters/Landov, 68
© Owaki/Kulla/CORBIS, 38
© Mark Peterson/CORBIS, 29
Joe Polillio/Getty Images, 15
© Mark Richards/CORBIS, 51, 59
Tim Shaffer/Reuters/Landov, 10
Chip Somodevilla/Getty Images, 45
Francis Specker/Landov, 37
Ramin Talaie/*Bloomberg News*/Landov, 63

About the Editor

Eleanor Stanford has an MA in English from the University of Wisconsin and an MFA in creative writing from the University of Virginia. Her poems have appeared in *Poetry, Ploughshares*, the *Georgia Review*, and other journals and anthologies. She lives in Philadelphia.